LOOKING BEYOND
THIS WORLD

LEVI W. RUSSELL

WESTBOW
PRESS®
A DIVISION OF THOMAS NELSON
& ZONDERVAN

WestBow Press books may be ordered through booksellers or by contacting:

WestBow Press
A Division of Thomas Nelson & Zondervan
1663 Liberty Drive
Bloomington, IN 47403
www.westbowpress.com
1 (866) 928-1240

Because of the dynamic nature of the Internet, any web addresses or
links contained in this book may have changed since publication and
may no longer be valid. The views expressed in this work are solely those
of the author and do not necessarily reflect the views of the publisher,
and the publisher hereby disclaims any responsibility for them.

Any people depicted in stock imagery provided by Thinkstock are
models, and such images are being used for illustrative purposes only.
Certain stock imagery © Thinkstock.

ISBN: 978-1-5127-3712-7 (sc)
ISBN: 978-1-5127-3713-4 (hc)
ISBN: 978-1-5127-3711-0 (e)

Library of Congress Control Number: 2016905416

Print information available on the last page.

WestBow Press rev. date: 10/11/2016

To our Lord and Savior, Jesus Christ,

my loving and supportive wife, Maudie, who

is the love of my life, and our son Philip.

PREFACE

As a boy, I tried to make something out of whatever material I could find. My brother, Rupert, who was older than me, always envied me. He would say, "Let me see what you have made." After I have showed it to him, he would not give it back to me, so a fight would ensue. I always would end up getting a whupping from him over my own things.

At an early age I went to Kingston, Jamaica, and there the Lord provided me with a job. It was a good job according to Jamaican standards, but it was not quite good enough for me. The Lord redirected my path to London, England. In England, the Lord provided a job for me working on the Tube. I became a train driver there. I planned to stay and settle down in London, England, but after nine and a half years on that job, the Lord told me to follow my wife and go to America. The Lord spoke, and so I obeyed.

We came to America on March 17, 1971, all three of us—my wife; our son John Russell, who was three years and three days old at that time; and I. In America we had another son whose name is Phillip. Here in America I began to knock at college doors in search of a higher education. I was accepted at Purchase College in Mount Vernon, New York. There at Purchase, the dean of the college asked me what I wanted to be when I finished college. I told her I wanted to be a preacher, an author, or a pharmacist. At the mentioning of writing books, one teacher commented, "Writing books!" and laughed; but here I am at the instruction of my Jesus, my Lord, and my God, trying to do just that. All things are possible for those who believe.

INTRODUCTION

I give credit to my Lord and Savior, Jesus Christ, who is the head of my life. My desire to write this book was an ambition that I kept pondering with in my mind ever so long, but the title of the book was what kept me in suspense. I asked the Lord if He would help me, and the answer was yes, but the title I had in my mind was wrong. So the Lord gave me the current title in my sleep one night, and I got up and wrote it down.

The problem with us human beings is that we are not concerned about our future life. Our eyes are so glued to this world that things taking place on other planets just do not faze us. Saint Paul declared that if it is only in this world we have hope, then we, of all men, will be most miserable. What is wrong with us is that we are not observant enough. The signs that Jesus spoke about are everywhere, but we do not stop to notice them. A case in point is that the dogs and elephants in Sumatra back in October 2010 knew that a Tsunami was coming and took to high ground, while men stood still in the time of the disaster, hence losing their lives.

The problems that the world is facing are selfishness, greed, and lust. And man does not accept the person of his fellow men. Peace and harmony will never be accomplished by man's efforts because the main ingredient, love, is not there. The prophet Jeremiah uttered that sentiment when he said, "It is not in you O man to order your own footsteps" (Jeremiah 10:23 KJV).

Presidents have a way of saying that they will do better than their predecessors, but instead things sometimes get worse under their administrations. The sooner we come to the realization that only God can fix earth's problems, the sooner we begin to look outside of this world for His help. As soon as we realize—like the psalmist David—that our help comes from the Lord, who made the heavens and the earth, the better off we will be. Our help is outside this world and not of this world.

Men in general are like babies. Babies' eyes are fixed bottles, and we don't ask them to look away. They would be upset if we did so because their only focus is on what is in the bottle. "Woe unto them that are with child, and to them that give suck in those days!" (Matthew 24:19). This world is so enticing to mankind that nothing else seems pleasing or can take its place. We are too confined to this world, and God wants us to reach out to Him because we walk by faith and not by sight, which leads me to my next subject—the knowledge of God.

CONTENTS

CHAPTER 1

THE KNOWLEDGE OF GOD

After I was converted and was baptized, I discovered that I loved the Lord in such a way that one Sunday night I went home from service and began to pray that the Lord would take me home to glory to be with Him that night, but God whispered to my heart and said, "Not tonight." I did not realize that I needed to be tested in order to have some testimonies. No test, no testimonies. Paul says, "If in this life only we have hope in Christ, we are of all men most miserable" (1 Corinthians 15:19). The phrase "If only in this world" signifies that there is another world to look forward to. We should not be so fascinated with this one that we lose sight of that which is to come.

When I decided to write this book, I asked the Lord about it because I wanted some money to buy a church but did not have enough funds. So the Lord said I should go ahead and write a book. He will help me. I asked the Lord what the title of the book should be. After a few weeks the Lord spoke to me in my sleep and said that the title of the book should be *Looking Beyond This World*. It was about 2:30 a.m., and I sprang off my bed and wrote it down, lest I should forget it.

I realize that many writers are concerned about things of this world, so they write according to the things of this world. They talk about this world, they live according to the way of this world, and they forge ahead according to what their eyes can see. But the Scripture says, "If ye be risen with Christ, then we should set our affections on things above and not on the things of this world" (Colossians 3:2). There is a brighter, better world above, awaiting all believers. All it takes to get there is faith in Jesus Christ.

I received my first knowledge of that world when I was about nine years old. I was a very sick child, and many people thought I wouldn't live. My brother and cousins called me many different names because of this, such as

Sick Fowl. Some of my problems still linger with me, but I won't divulge them. But out of my weakness comes my strength. I died, and my father, who was at my bedside, did not even know it. One conclusion that I have to come to is that all children that have not been tampered with belong to the Lord Jesus Christ. Therefore, at the second coming of the Lord, those that are with child and the parents of young children will weep because their children will go missing. They will be raptured.

CHAPTER 2

NEAR-DEATH EXPERIENCE

An experience I had as a child makes me realize that young children will be escorted before their parents' eyes, and mothers and fathers can do nothing about it. Jeremiah wrote that Rachel cried for her children and could not be comforted, for her children were not comforted.

Herod destroyed them through jealousy, lust, and outrage for power. But our God is going to save them through love, saving them from the wrath to come. He knew that they had done nothing wrong to deserve the flames of fire in hell.

My soul left my body and went up and up and up. What word can I use to describe the speed at which my soul traveled? It passed planets at lightning speed, and in a moment I was in a new world. The world was as real as this one, only it was perfect. There was no pain, no hunger, no thirst, no sorrow, and no night. Jesus was the light there. There was an entrance, and I entered through it. I found myself standing before a man who was seated at a table; I suppose he was Father Abraham. His countenance was pleasant, his color was golden bronze, and he was seated at a golden table. It is very hard to explain. I was just a child. He barely looked at me and said, "Go back; it's not your time."

I then turned around and started my descent back to earth, but I must describe the place I saw. It was a beautiful place where the grass was all green and the trees were all young and green. As far as I could see were green pastures, but I did not see any fruit on any of the trees; nor did I see any animals. Saint Paul said it well when he said, "That eyes have not seen nor ears heard neither hath it entered in the hearts of men the things the Lord hath prepared for them that love Him" (1 Corinthians 2:9).

The songwriter Isaac Watts wrote these lyrics from the song, "Am I a soldier of the cross" reminds me of this encounter.

Must I be carried to the skies

On flowery beds of ease,

While others fought to win the prize,

and sailed through the bloody seas?

CHAPTER 3

RETURN TO MY BODY

Upon returning to my body, the first voice I heard was that of my cousin's wife, Gwendolyn. She was about eighteen years older than I was. She said, "Uncle D [my father's name was David], I told you that Levi was not born to stay in this world!" My dad's reply to her was "Leave him; he will live!" The mistake many churches are making is suggesting that God is not in the healing business anymore.

Of course I said nothing to either my cousin or my dad. I kept everything to myself and pondered it in my heart. What this experience has taught me is that the body is a different entity from the soul. The body cannot exist without the soul, but the soul can and will exist without the body.

Peter declared that he must put off the tabernacle as the Lord had showed him. I am one that had taken my flight to the world above. Jesus spoke a parable about Lazarus and the rich man, as recorded in Luke 16:19–31. Lazarus died and was taken into Abraham's bosom, and the rich man died also and found himself in hell. The rich man looked up from hell and saw Lazarus in Abraham's bosom; he requested that Abraham send Lazarus to him and that he be allowed to dip his finger in water to quench his thirst, but that request was denied. The second request was that he be sent to warn his brethren so that they might believe in him after he came back from the dead, but that request was denied also. His brethren had Moses and Elias, and if they did not believe not Moses and Elias, they would not believe someone who had returned from the dead.

The point I am trying to make is this: here our Lord Jesus spoke of the reality of heaven and hell. He instructed His disciples to write about it to let everyone know about it. Why is Abraham in charge of that world? The answer is that he is the father of faith, and without faith it is impossible to please God.

CHAPTER 4

HOW I GOT SAVED

It was a Friday night in 1957, and my girlfriend and I had plans to go to a dance that we had been looking forward to for some time. She was to leave from her job and head straight to the dance. I was going to meet her there, but when I arrived, she wasn't there yet. The place was so packed that I decided to go up to a nearby church to pass the time until she arrived. At the church were two women—evangelists from America who were conducting a revival meeting. The message of the night piqued my interest, so I decided to stay instead of going back to the dance. The sermon was about Jesus of Nazareth passing by a sycamore tree and looking up and seeing Zacchaeus. Jesus told to him to hurry and come down, and He told him He must stay at Zacchaeus's house. That sermon touched my heart because all Jesus wants is to abide in our hearts.

After the sermon there was an altar call. Everyone went up to the altar except for me. I do not recall which of the two evangelists came over to me while I had my head bowed, but she held me by my shirtsleeve and said, "You bright-faced young man, you need Jesus." She then led me to the altar. While I was going, I was laughing because I had no intention at that moment of committing myself to the Lord. However, when I reached the altar and knelt down and began to pray, something came into my heart. Joy filled my soul. I cried and praised God. When the meeting was over and I passed the dance to go home, I passed the place as if nothing were going on there that would be of any interest to me. I was saved! The Lord took charge of my life.

The next day, when I met up with the young lady I was to meet at the dance, she inquired as to what had happened to me that kept me from showing up. I told her that I had been saved, and she laughed at me with scorn. From that day forward, our friendship was severed. The

Lord told me to leave the parish of St. Elizabeth and head to Kingston, the capital of Jamaica. I never spoke to that young lady again. Looking back to that night, it seems as if I were Zacchaeus and Jesus wanted to come into my heart. I am so happy that I let Him.

CHAPTER 5

THE REVELATION OF THE THREE-IN-ONE GOD

In the year 1958 I was employed by J Ray & Nephew Bottling Co. in Jamaica. Every day after work, as soon as I reached home, my first priority was to kneel and pray. On one particular day after riding my bicycle to and from a very hard day of work, I was so tired I threw myself down across the bed and fell fast asleep. I don't know how long I was asleep, but there came over me three identical persons; their glory cannot be described. My only description is that they were three amber lights shining like the sun. It was not possible to differentiate them. All I know is that the one in the middle stretched out his hand, touched me on my belly, shook me three times, and said, "Peter! Could you not watch with me one hour?"

Immediately I woke from my sleep, fell on my knees, and began to cry and pray, knowing that I had just had the highest form of visitation in this universe in my humble little abode. What could a young Christian want more than that—the great God of the universe identifying Himself to sinful man?

What this revelation did for me was confirm the words of Jesus, my Lord and Master, that He, the Holy Spirit, and His Father are one. He also said that if one has seen Him, he or she has seen the Father also. He said as well that He does nothing of Himself, but only those things He sees His Father do. So in the case of Jesus, it's only the flesh that the Father, Son, and Holy Spirit used to disguise Him. I use the term "three-in-one God," also known as the Trinity because they are one and the same. You can see all three standing together and say "God!"

"He that hath not the Father, hath not the Son also" (1 John 2:23). For that reason, no one should argue with the people who do not believe in the Trinity. It is only that their spiritual eyes have not been illuminated, for at least they have believed in someone who is of the Godhead.

In my case, who was it that placed His hands on me and shook me and spoke those words? Was it the Father, the Son, or was He the Holy Spirit? I will never be able to say. All that I can say is that He was God.

Why should we think that anything is impossible with God? It is He who has made man with such vast potential. Why should we think His potential is limited? "'I am Alpha and Omega, the beginning and the end, the first and the last,' says the Lord" (Revelation 1:8).

CHAPTER 6

LOOKING BEYOND
THIS WORLD

The apostle Philip asked the Lord to show them the Father, saying that would suffice for them, but Jesus' reply was "Have I been so long with you and you have not known me, Philip? He that hath seen me hath seen the Father also" (John 14:9).

Too many people pretend to know more about God than what Jesus, our Lord, knows. We can well understand why God did not require anyone to come up to Mount Sinai to receive the instructions and commandments from Him, except Moses.

If He had asked for Aaron and Miriam to come up with Moses, what a contradiction and confusion we would have today. There would be a lot of bickering—perhaps protests as well—and denial concerning what took place and what God said. But the face of Moses alone shone, bearing witness that he was alone in the presence of God and no other. God had to hush up Miriam by giving her leprosy because she wanted to share leadership with Moses.

The revelation of the triune God will convince you that there are three Gods in one. In my vision I saw the three Gods bonded at the waist; there was one body with three heads. God was revealing to me that what I had been taught by the Church of Christ was wrong. God is really a three-in-one God.

Man's biggest problem is that he has failed to believe that God is a revealer of all secrets to all who diligently seek Him. The moment many get saved, they are presented with a plan of how to be prosperous materially and not spiritually.

The Scripture says that we should seek first the kingdom of heaven and all its righteousness, and that if we do so, all things will be added unto us; but man has switched that around to make it say, "Seek first the world, and all things will be added unto you."

Many are seeking the creation and not the Creator, which becomes a snare instead of a blessing. For what is our life? It's like a vapor; it appears for a little while and then vanishes, and what then?

CHAPTER 7

FATHER, SON, AND HOLY GHOST

The criterion of entering into God's kingdom is the Holy Spirit. For the Scripture says that he who has not the Spirit of God is none of His. (See Romans 8:9). God is a Spirit, and they who worship Him must do so in spirit and in truth. Now the contention is, how much of His spirit do we embody? For if we embody more of the world than of the Holy Spirit; we are not worthy of Him.

Nicodemus, a Jew who came to Him desiring to know more about Him and the kingdom of heaven, was told that he must be born again. There are those who are teaching that one can get to heaven without the Holy Spirit. This is like saying one can get to the moon without a rocket.

We are reliant on earth's atmosphere; we cannot survive without oxygen. So much for that thought.

Secondly, we must all be changed in the twinkling of an eye. Who and what is going to change us? Who is going to quicken us? We have to be quickened by the Holy Spirit of God. The flesh cannot quicken anything. If a piece of flesh is on or beside another piece of flesh, those pieces of flesh cannot quicken one another or bring life to one another; they are just dead flesh. It is the Spirit that quickens, or makes things alive. It is time for the church to establish what God's priority is instead of what man's priority is. God's priority is that we should seek first the kingdom of heaven and all its righteousness, and all things will then be added unto us. Man's priority is that we should seek first material things, which leaves us empty and void.

It was more appropriate in the heart of Adam to carry out the Devil's mandate than to carry out God's mandate, for the Devil's advice appeals to the satisfaction of the flesh. But for Christians it should not be so, for we are told that "Man shall not live by bread alone but by every word that proceedeth out of the mouth of God" (Matthew 4:4).

For anyone to venture into outer space, one must take all the necessary precautions because it not a territory that is conducive to the flesh; but the earth is conducive to the flesh because we are fallen creatures.

Yet as man we have a second chance because of what our Lord Jesus Christ has done for us. His instructions say we must be born again. They that are born of the flesh are just flesh, but they that are born of the Spirit are of the Spirit. (See Romans 8:5). Flesh and blood cannot inherit eternal life. I believe, therefore, that man's greatest problem is that he has placed too much emphasis on the flesh. We do practically everything to draw attention to the flesh. Man's evaluation of the flesh exceeds anyone's belief or expectation. In other words, we are living in a world of make-believe.

What is interesting to me is that when sickness sets in for a man or woman who lives after the will of the flesh, he or she asks for prayer, wanting God to heal the flesh that is so rebellious against God. The Spirit must heal the flesh, while the flesh is so rebellious against the Spirit. "God is a Spirit, and they that worship Him must do so in spirit and in truth" (John 4:24).

CHAPTER 8

JACKA CHRISTIANITY

As a young man, I used to play cricket. Thirteen young men would show up to play the game, but there were only six men to a team, and the thirteenth man would be referred to as a "jacka." A jacka is known in Jamaica as a person that can play on both sides. When the game is over, no matter which side is victorious, the jacka claims victory as well. God does not appreciate jacka Christianity. No one can serve two masters; you must cling to one and despise the other. (See Romans 12:9.) You cannot serve God and mammon. There are many who play the role of the jacka in the church. They worship God and the Devil. They're unaware that God does not appreciate them in their double roles in the church.

CHAPTER 9

INTRODUCTION OF THE CHURCH AGE

I had another vision of a milling crowd, and they were of the church age, for out of that church age there were just a few that were going up a narrow pathway, and the others were going on a broad way, not looking where they were going. As they all passed me, I heard the tumbling and crying out of the people that were falling into a pit on the broad way. And when I turned around, I saw the others that were coming from the world's direction; they had no way of escaping the pit. As the Scripture says, "Broad is the way that leads to destruction and so many enter in thereat. Narrow is the path that leads in life so few have found it" (Matthew 7:13). We should not assume that everyone that says,

"Lord! Lord!" will enter into heaven. Those who do not live a Christian life and accept the Lord Jesus Christ as their Lord and Savior would be better off never to have been born. (See Matthew 26:24).

CHAPTER 10

MY FLIGHT OVER HELL

In my vision, hell is not a place underneath earth. Hell is a separate place west of this earth. As I was out of my body and flying over hell, I saw Satan in a deep, deep valley, and he was flogging the souls of men. Satan was dressed in black clothing. He had a whip, and even though the souls were trying to get away by crawling from between his legs, he was still flogging them. I wondered how one could escape him because he was a big man. He seemed to be the master of his business. I thought to myself how impossible it would be for one who entered hell to get out, except for God.

I looked farther out. There was a big fire in the distance, and I supposed that fire was there awaiting judgment day. When I woke out of my sleep and discovered that what

I had just witnessed was just a vision, I was glad. While there I felt I was dead. And I could see I had no feet in my vision; I had only wings. My only means of light was a burning candle that I carried in my left hand; in my right hand I carried my rod, for protection. When I woke up, I was pondering what had taken place.

The next vision I had was of the Lord taking me into his abode in the heavens, where I saw the Lord's back but not his face. I was so excited with the place that I kept looking at his back. It was the image of a lamb. I am not certain if the place was a painting or if it was the sky. I was so amazed at the beauty of this place and of being in the presence of the Lord. The Lord turned his side to me and said, "You say that you love me, but you do not trust me!"

I replied, "Yes, Lord, I trust you."

He repeated Himself: "You say that you love me, but you do not trust me!"

I declared again, "Yes, Lord, I trust you!"

When I was back in my body about a week later, the Lord took me to hell. The very place that I had felt uncomfortable about entering was where the Lord took me. The very spot where I had seen Satan flogging the life out of the souls of men was where I found myself. There I saw Satan's throne. It was just a big stone. The Lord brought out to me a white couple that I knew from Jamaica, Mr. and Mrs. Lynch. I said to them, "What are you two people doing in this place, where there is no hope of escaping?"

They both answered, saying, "God did it because we would not obey Him. He placed us down here."

I said to them, "Because I obey Him, I now have a home in heaven." After saying those words, it was like an engine started up, and I was out of hell in a moment. I was back in my body again. My passage over hell was a result of the instrument the Lord gave me to fly and observe what was going on down in hell.

Hell did not appear to be an old place. In my opinion, it was made after Satan in heaven and was thrown out. God prepared a place to put him and those that rebelled with him. (See Ezekiel 28) Hell was made in a hurry, and there is no beauty about it. It is a place where broken stones are on the ground because there is nowhere else to place them.

From my vantage point I had a panoramic view, and I could see fire in the distance. Satan was nowhere to be seen. The place was in total darkness except for the light that was around me. Satan had to take flight because Jesus was with me. Jesus is the light of the world, and whoever walks with Him will never walk in darkness but will have the light of life. (See John 8:12). Jesus spoke and told John that he should not fear for he was alive and was dead and is alive forevermore. Jesus has the keys for death and hell. (See Revelation1:18). And the psalmist David said, "Yea though I walk through the valley and the shadow of death I will fear no evil for thou are with me thy rod and thy staff they comfort me thou preparest a table before me in presence of my enemies" (Psalm 23).

There I saw two women in long dresses walking on top of the large broken stones. They were talking to each other but looked very distressed. My concern was not with the ladies; their backs were turned to me, and I couldn't hear their conversation. It was made clear to me that the reason

I was there was for the couple I mentioned earlier—the Lynches. God was telling me that disobedience to Him will make one go to hell. In Luke 6:46 the Lord said, "Why call ye me, Lord Lord and do not the things, which I say?" This scripture is fitting because the Lynches should have known better, but chose to be disobedient to the words of God.

CHAPTER 11

POPULAR OPINION OF THE RELIGIOUS SECTS

The popular opinion of many religious sects is that once you are saved, you cannot be lost. That may sound good to many, but realistically that does not hold true with God. Jesus said that we should take heed unto ourselves lest our hearts be overcharged with surfeiting. Surfeiting means indulging to the point of satiety, whatever that indulgence might be.

The love of money is the root of all evil. One might say that the lottery is a government-sponsored operation and it is lawful to participate in it. However, it is not lawful according to God's law. Saint Paul wrote in 1 Corinthians 10:23 that although all things are lawful for him, all things are not expedient; all things that are of the law are not good. If we blatantly break God's laws down here, so will we want to break God's laws up there. There are those preachers that say God does not love one less than others whether one has sinned or not. But Jesus did not say so. Jesus said there are those that will say unto Him, "Did I not prophesy in your name and perform many miracles?" And He will say, "Depart from me ye that work inequity, you evildoers. I know you not." (See Matthew 7:22–23.)

CHAPTER 12

A JOURNEY THROUGH THE WILDERNESS

The Lord took me on a journey through the wilderness. I was alone in a small vehicle, and I was bound for the pearly gates. In the wilderness were trees, stones, and all kind of obstacles to prevent the vehicle from going forward. At times I had to step out and clear the way for the vehicle, but I alone was in the vehicle. I often thought my vehicle would shut off at times, but I still continued on to the pearly gates. I did not stop; I went on and on until finally I reached the pearly gates. There I stood behind a man. I did not know who the person was.

One of the disciples told me I should come around from behind this man, and when I went inside to change my clothes, I looked back to see who this person was, and it was Clement Levy. He had his own church in Jamaica. I said to him, "I know you!" And he said to me, "I know you, too." I was woken out of my sleep in that instant. I pondered the whole situation, as he had died a year and a half before.

The following day I phoned Jamaica to ask a friend of ours what kind of preacher he was, and the friend said he was no good. She began to remind me of what he had done to my grandmother, my mother, and even to me. I remember that he took away our land that my grandmother had been paying taxes for. I remember a day when he took his cows, goats, and donkeys and tied them up on our land and they destroyed our cultivation. When he was asked why he was doing this, his reply was that the land had not been given to my grandmother forever but was only to be hers for a time.

However, my grandmother had worked as a nurse for his grandfather when he became ill. The piece of land our house was built on had been given to her as a reward for her care for him. Her name was on the tax roll, and she was paying taxes for the land. We had three houses and two kitchens on that land. It was where I was born and where I lived until I was a teenager. Clement Levy later sold the land, and he died a few years later.

According to the Scriptures (Luke 19:1–10), the Lord went to Zacchaeus's house to eat and drink with him, and Zacchaeus stood up and said, "Lord if I had taken anything from any man falsely I restore unto him four fold." And the Lord said unto him "Even today has salvation come unto your house?" Zacchaeus returned fourfold unto every man that he had robbed the things he had taken from them.

Clement Levy did not do what Zacchaeus did by returning or repaying what he had taken. Therefore, this could be the reason why I saw him still standing at heaven's pearly gates; perhaps he could not enter because he did not repent or try to undo his wrongs.

There are many preachers today that have taken that path. They covet a man's wife and will not stop until the marriage is dissolved. And then they act as if they are not responsible for the breaking up of the marriage. We should not think that one can escape God's judgment.

One may think he or she has gotten away with that kind of behavior on earth, but not up there. The book will be open. Whether it affects one or not, one should not think he will not be held accountable for his behavior.

CHAPTER 13

THE HUMAN CHARTER

The human charter is the written agreement between God and man. These laws (i.e., the Bible) are used to guide men in their daily affairs. We may not consider that God is instructing us and keeping us in our human affairs, but if God had taken away His charter, scarcely anyone would be saved. There is another force that is trying to destroy men, and had it not been for the help of God, we would all be destroyed. There are those that feel that the violence in the world, especially in the schools, does not amount to anything, but God has taken away His charter. His Spirit has been withdrawn from these people who commit these violent acts. The natural disasters, such as the hurricanes, floods, and tsunamis that the world is experiencing in the present day, are indications that God has withdrawn

Himself from the human charter, just as in the days of Noah and the mighty flood. God gave Noah instructions on building the ark and securing His people and animals of every kind. Unfortunately the people ignored Noah's warnings, and when the flood came, they realized Noah had been telling the truth; but by then it was too late, and they perished.

Another example is men removing God's charter from public schools. The Bible and its readings, the Ten Commandments, and prayer are no longer present in the schools. So God in turn has removed Himself from the schools. Hence violence, teen pregnancy, drug use, and all manner of unruliness have taken over. Galatians 6:8 states that whoever sows to the flesh shall reap corruption; but whoever sows to the Spirit shall reap life eternal. Jesus came so that we may have life through His name.

I believe that the expiration of the human charter is in effect right now. The doors of mercy are closing gradually. Unless one is converted and becomes as a little child, he or she cannot enter the kingdom of God. Once the Master of the House arises and shuts the door, they that are without shall begin to weep and mourn and ask for God's mercy. Some will ask on that day, "Why did God close the door on us?" The answer will be "Why not! We had it our way for thousands of years while God was speaking, and now God is going to have it His way. Few took heed to what God had to say and responded."

One may say to me that the churches have a lot of people in them, and I will reply that those people are a mixture of wheat and tares. (See Matthew 13:24–30.) Moreover, God is not looking for quantity but quality, just as Matthew 25 explains about the ten virgins. Five of them were wise, and five were foolish.

The Holy Spirit has been withdrawn little by little, and the demonic spirit is taking over evangelical preachers. The Scripture Romans 1:28 says that because they would not retain God in their hearts, God gave them over to their reprobate minds to live in their filthy ways—men with men, women with women—and there is no end to the filthiness.

The first charter between God and man was with Adam and Eve, when He told them, "The day that you eat the fruit of this tree, you shall die." And they disobeyed God and paid bitterly for their disobedience. They could no longer enter the garden of Eden to partake in the fruits thereof.

I must confess that many of the prosperity sermons in our day sound good, but is that what God wants us to proclaim? I do not believe so, but rather we should be speaking like Jehu to the messengers of Jezebel. They asked Jehu whether it was peace, and Jehu replied, "What has peace to do with me? So long as the sins of Jezebel continue, there will be no peace. Get thee behind me." There can be no peace in this world as long as the sins of the world continue.

The Holy Spirit spoke through me on July 4, 2012 and said that the human charter has ended. This means that the partnership that God has with man is no more. The evidence of this was seen when hurricane Sandy hit the Northeast in October 2012, when the school shooting took place at Sandy Hook Elementary in December 2012, and in other events thereafter.

As soon as a child is born, he or she is introduced to ball games and other sports activities and not to the Word of God. And we wonder why the children are so violent and obnoxious toward one another. The reason why is as the psalmist David said: "Where withal shall a young man cleanse his ways but by taking heed to the word of God" (Psalm 119:9).

I understand this will be an area of disagreement by many, but as Jeremiah said to King Jehoiakim and the people of his day, "If my head was water and my eyes were a fountain I would weep day and night for the destruction of my people Israel" (Jeremiah 9:1).

What leaves us in spiritual darkness today is the doctrine of eternal security, which says once one is saved, he or she cannot be lost.

CHAPTER 14

MY ENCOUNTER WITH THE BURIAL GROUND

In a vision, the Lord caused me to go through a portion of a burial ground in Jamaica. I saw many people sitting top of their tombs. I shouted to them, "Say, 'Praise the Lord!'" I repeated myself three times, saying "Say, 'Praise the Lord!'" There was no response from the crowd of people. I woke up and said to myself, "What a fool am I." As the prophet Isaiah and the psalmist David said, "For the grave cannot praise thee, death can [not] celebrate thee: they that go down into the pit cannot hope for thy truth.""The dead praise not the Lord, neither any that go down into silence." Only the living can declare their truth only the living can praise you (Isaiah 38:18, Psalm 115:17).

Many Christians do not know how important it is to worship and praise the Lord. Many are more willing to praise ballplayers than the great God of the universe. The Devil laughs when we are worshipping the creature rather than the Creator, who is blessed forevermore. It's unthinkable that one should believe that God, the creator of all things, should create a nice place for the Enemy to enjoy rather than a place of regret. The men or women that think they do not have to praise God down here on earth and want to wait until they reach heaven are sadly mistaken, for whatever we do down here will take us to one place or the other.

David declares on several occasions that men are to praise the Lord. For example, see Psalms 145–150. We are to praise Him for what he has done: the air we breathe, the water we drink, our health and strength, the food we eat, the clothes we wear, all our amenities, and most of all His act of salvation. We need to glorify His name. The dead cannot praise Him; only the living can. We need to take our rightful place and not allow the stones to cry out for us. Jesus said, "If these children will not praise Him the stones will cry out" (Luke 19:37–40). God has made us with voices and hearts to praise Him.

CHAPTER 15

A PLACE OF REST

I will begin by saying that all of God's people have a place of rest. God made it especially for them. He has kept them by families; for example, the family of Jacob was kept in Goshen, apart from the family of Egypt.

I was taken by the Spirit of God into the graves of our beloved relatives. The first grave we went to was my uncle Stanley's place of rest. I reminisced about the last conversation we had, and I spoke to him about accepting the Lord Jesus Christ as his Lord and Savior and the soon-coming King. He was very reluctant in repeating the confession of faith after me. He finally did, and he died shortly after. When I entered his grave, he had his back turned to me, standing in darkness. He was frightened when I called out to him. Uncle Stanley looked very sad. He did not say a word to me, so I left.

The next graves I visited were the graves of my mother-in-law and father-in-law. There were three spirits in a lighted space; a young man was occupying the space with them. I could not recognize who this young man was, but they were all contented, and we conversed for a moment; but when I was leaving, I asked them, "Have you heard from Jesus as of yet?"

They all shouted enthusiastically at the same time, "Yes! We have heard from Jesus."

I said to them, "Good for you. You are blessed!" I can assure you they were Christians while they were living on earth.

Preaching the gospel of Jesus Christ while you are still living makes all the difference in one's final resting place. The believer is the light representing Jesus Christ; He is the light of the world. Jesus will never leave us in darkness, but the Devil will. And the Lord has promised us He will never leave us or forsake us. He will always come to us.

CHAPTER 16

JESUS'S POTENTIAL

My wife and I were praising God one Saturday morning, and after we prayed I felt tired. So I went to take a nap, and while I was sleeping the Holy Spirit said unto me, "You are going to see Jesus just as He was on earth." In the same moment, Jesus appeared. He looked like any ordinary man, but I could see He was extraordinary. He smiled at me, and I was frightened when I saw Him. When I awoke from my sleep, I began to worship Him. I wondered what Isaiah had said about Him when he saw Jesus. "He grew up before him like a tender plant and like a root out of the ground. He had no beauty or majesty to attract us to him—nothing in his appearance that would cause us to desire him. He was despised and rejected by mankind, a man of suffering familiar with pain. Like one from whom people hide their faces, he was despised, and we held him in low esteem". (Isaiah 53:2–3).

I wondered whom Isaiah was referring to because in my estimation Jesus was beautiful. Isaiah must have been speaking of His execution on the cross because there they brutally beat Him. He could not seem beautiful after what they did to Him. Even as Jesus lay on the cross He said He would rise on the third day, and He did so. Praise God!

We can always take Jesus at His word. For example, Mary, His mother, knew so much about Him that when they were in Galilee at a wedding that ran out of wine, Mary told the people that they should do whatever Jesus said unto them. It appeared that His potential was limitless because the word made Him limitless. Jesus would be true to His word. They followed His direction by filling pots with water, and they poured out perfect wine. (See John 2:1–11.) Jesus said to the people that Lazarus was not dead but would rise again. Who else could have said such words and made it happen? (See John 11:1–45) Jesus's potential was limitless because He was able to take a child's lunch of three barley loaves and three small fish and feed a multitude of five thousand. (See Matthew 14:13–21).

CHAPTER 17

THE GLORIFIED NAME OF JESUS IS REVEALED

It is true that with the name of Jesus all things are possible to him that believes because Jesus is God Himself. We have God the Father, God the Son, and God the Holy Ghost. He came down to earth to dwell among men, and the Father had to withhold some of His power—for example, the power to create; He did not come down here with the power to create man or create a new world. However, the Father gave Him enough power to convince those who would believe that He is the Son of God. There is enough evidence to support His being the Son of God, but this can only come by faith in the Lord Jesus Christ.

"When He was resurrected and appeared to ten of His disciples in an upper room, Thomas was not there and Judas had already evicted himself. When Thomas came, the Lord was not there, and the ten said, "The other disciples therefore said unto him, We have seen the Lord. But he said unto them, Except I shall see in his hands the print of the nails, and put my finger into the print of the nails, and thrust my hand into his side, I will not believe.

And after eight days again his disciples were within, and Thomas with them: [then] came Jesus, the doors being shut, and stood in the midst, and said, "Peace be unto you".

27 Then saith he to Thomas, Reach hither thy finger, and behold my hands; and reach hither thy hand, and thrust [it] into my side: and be not faithless, but believing. (John 20:25–27 KJV).

So you see, there are many facets to Jesus. One moment He could come through an open door, and in the next He could come through a locked door. There is no telling what God can or will do. All we have to do is believe in Jesus and have faith in Him. Praise the Lord!

CHAPTER 18

MY LIFE IN ENGLAND

In pursuit of a better life I left Jamaica and settled in London, England, in 1961. I landed a job at a candy factory, but the wage from that job was so small in comparison to what I had been making in Jamaica that I was struggling to survive financially. I used to cry out to the Lord to ask how I was to make a living off of the small salary. I left the candy factory to join the London Transport Executive as a platform sweeper. Although the pay was the same, the opportunity for growth was there. I soon moved into the role of being a train guard. I was a guard for two years, but the pay was still inadequate. I began searching for a new place of employment that would meet my salary requirements, but I could not find anything.

One Monday night I cried out to the Lord for guidance, and He spoke to me that night and advised me to stay where I was and not to leave the job. One night as I was praying to the Lord and asking Him for a better job, the Lord said to me in a loud voice, "Go into all the world and preach the gospel, and lo I am with you always."

About two months after the Lord spoke to me, I received a letter from the London Transport Board asking if I would like to become a train driver. The stationmaster did not encourage me to accept the offer, because he did not feel I had enough experience to be promoted to a train driver. The driver of the train I had been guarding for the past two years knew I was capable, and he told me to sign the offer. And so I did.

After accepting the position, I was sent to attend The London Underground Training School to become a train driver. For three weeks I learned signaling, the different parts of the train, and the operations of the train in the event that something broke down. I met a colleague from Barbados who was also going to this school. Griffith had been going to this school for years. He was trying

Looking Beyond This World

to learn everything about the train so that he could pass the exam to become a train driver. When Griffith finally took the exam and failed, everyone—including me—was disheartened to know that someone who was so dedicated to learning all about the train and who knew so much had failed the test.

I went home and cried unto the Lord, asking, "If Griffith failed, how can I pass?" I was really comparing myself to Griffith. The Lord spoke to me that Saturday night and said in a very loud voice, "Am I not God and not able to help you?" His voice was so loud that I was sure everyone in the building heard Him. I thought that someone would say something to me the next day, but no one did. From then on I thought the Lord's voice was powerful enough to wake the dead.

I went to church that Sunday morning, and when the pastor got up from the pulpit to speak, he said this was not his originally prepared sermon, but just the night before the Lord had come to him and said to tell the people, "Am I not God? Am I not able to help you?" When I heard this I broke down and began to cry because I knew that message was intended for me because of the words the Lord had spoken to me just the night before. That same week, the Lord allowed me to drive the train with an experienced train driver who was going to the school to become an instructor. His name was Mr. Humphrey. While I drove the train, Mr. Humphrey asked me what I did not understand about the train, saying he would explain it to me. I informed him that I did not understand how the air flowed through the brake system. Mr. Humphrey was very diligent in showing me how the brake system worked on the train. My eyes were opened to the truth. Mr. Humphrey urged me to go home to continue to study. At the time of my exam, I was able to thoroughly explain to the examiner all of the functions of the train. I passed the exam with flying colors. "God is the strength of my life and my light of whom shall I fear" (Psalm 73:26).

God changed my life, and from that point on there were no more struggles.

There I became a member of a Pentecostal church. I began to study the Bible and was soon able to read the Scriptures. By doing so I developed a very good understanding of the Bible. Under the Lord's direction at that church in 1965, I met and married my wife, Maude.

My wife and I welcomed our firstborn son, John, on March 14, 1968. John was a very happy baby, but he was constantly plagued with health issues. My wife wanted to move from England to America to see if the change in environment would improve John's health, but I wanted to stay in England. To convince my wife to stay in England, I thought it would be a good idea to purchase a home. After looking at several houses, we found one that would suit our needs. Even though it needed a lot of repairs, we liked it. The previous owner had left the house to her four children. I was already approved for a mortgage, so we made an offer, but two of the children rejected it. In order for the house to be sold, all of the children would have to agree on the selling price. My wife and I prayed to ask the Lord for guidance.

We negotiated for months, and we finally reached an agreement. We were happy that we were going to be homeowners. Nights before I was to sign for the loan, the Lord appeared to me. He was suspended in the air with

His arms outstretched right over the road I would have to drive on to go to the mortgage office. He said to me with a loud voice, "I am the Lord thy God. I am against the way you are going. Follow your wife and go to America."

This vision left me puzzled. I did not disclose the vision I had to my wife. I was worried what the sellers and the people at the mortgage company would say if I backed out now. So I concocted a plan that made sense to me. Since I was approved for a mortgage and we both loved the house, I would buy the house, fix it up to resell it, and then move to America. The day I had to go to close on the loan, I drove the very route the Lord had showed me in the vision. I kept looking up to see if I could see Him. When I finally reached the mortgage company, a lady there informed me that the city council had suspended the loan program until the following year. Even though I was already approved, I would not be able to get the loan until the following year. I took the stairs to exit the building, and on my way down I began to sing:

All the way my Savior leads me;

what have I to ask beside?

Can I doubt His tender mercy, who

through life has been my guide?

Heavenly peace, divinest comfort,

Here by faith in Him to dwell!

For I know, whatever befall me,

Jesus doeth all things well.

CHAPTER 19

COMING TO AMERICA

When I arrived back home, I told my wife about the mortgage situation and then told her of the dream I had of the Lord directing me to follow her and go to America. She was elated. That same day, my wife, our son, and I went down to the embassy to file for our visas to come to America. And the papers came through very fast. In less than four months, we were approved. In March of 1971, we were off to the United States, where we landed in New York at John F. Kennedy airport.

My wife was able to continue her career as a registered nurse after passing her nursing exams in America. I, on the other hand, was not as fortunate, so my wife had to assume the responsibility of being the main source of income during this time. After working a few ill-fated jobs, the Lord showed me in a vision that I must stand up on a big rock and allow my wife to pass me a long rod to reach high-hanging breadfruit, a staple food product of Jamaica. From the vision I knew that Jesus was the rock and my wife passing me the rod signified her providing the money for me to go to a trade school in Manhattan to learn about air-conditioning and refrigeration.

After attending the trade school and receiving my certification, I was not able to find a job in this field. In a vision the Lord showed me that I must study for my next job. So I took up my books and studied. I phoned the school to inform them that I was not working. The school advised me of two possible job openings that I was qualified for, but they were located outside the state of New York. One was in New Jersey, and the other in Connecticut. I did not know how to reach either of them, but in my travels I had seen highway signs that showed the way to Connecticut, so I informed the school that I was interested in interviewing for the position in Connecticut.

The school provided me with an address and a time to show up. At the time, I did not know what the job entailed, but I found out when I arrived that the job was for a heating and air-conditioning technician at the Southern New England Telephone Company. A young lady who said I would be a good candidate for the job interviewed me, but she also let me know that they still had eleven other people to interview. I felt the interview went well, but I left feeling uncertain that I would get the job. I received a letter a week later requesting that I come in for a second interview; this interview would be conducted by a superintendent and a foreman to confirm I was qualified for the job by asking technical questions.

Before leaving the interview I was informed they were still interviewing, but they said I would be contacted by them to let me know their decision. After I left that day, the Lord showed me He was going to give me the job. You see how the Lord works. "Trust in the Lord with all your heart, and lean not on thine own understanding. In all thy ways acknowledge Him and He will direct thy paths" (Proverbs 3:5–6).

CHAPTER 20

THE CALL OF GOD ON MY LIFE TO PREACH THE GOSPEL

When I was in England, I kept praying to God to bless me. The Lord came one night and said in a loud voice, "Go into all the world and preach the gospel and lo I am with you always" (Matthew 28:20).

The first time I was called to preach, I cried because I had never been to Bible school or received formal training in ministry. However, the Lord came along and gave me the first sermon. He also gave me a vision that I was swimming in deep waters out in the ocean, although I could not swim. There were two men helping me, one on my right and one on my left. I woke out of my sleep and realized that God was with me and He would help me to preach the gospel.

The Sunday evening when I preached my first sermon, there was one sister, Sister Brown, who said I blessed her soul. Other people began to comment on how my sermon blessed their souls. However, the pastor of the church was angry with them. He said, "Brother Russell preaches one little sermon, and everyone is happy and commenting on how the message blessed their souls. And when I preach, no one comments, nor is there anyone giving me any accolades on my sermon!" From that point on he would no longer give me opportunities to preach in his pulpit. The Lord had shown me the way already.

CHAPTER 21

MY REVELATION

My revelation to you, my dear reader, is that I had a daughter when I was young, before I got saved or married. My daughter, Patricia, was born in Jamaica. When I moved to England, she stayed with her mother in Jamaica. After I was married, my wife and I discussed the possibilities of bringing Patricia to live with us in England. After a time we decided that we would postpone sending for Patricia to move to England because we were making preparations for our move to the United States. Patricia was delighted to hear the news that we were going to America. She said, "Dad that is where I want to go."

After living in America for two years, my family and I went back to Jamaica on vacation and saw Patricia and her mother. They both were very humble. We spent a lot of time together because our hotel was very near to their home. Every place we went, Patricia was with us. There was no request too great for Patricia or her mother to fill for my family or me. They both showed us the utmost respect. So we knew from this visit that there would be no issues with Patricia coming to live with us in America.

A short time after Patricia arrived in America, my wife and I began to regret our decision. We found it difficult to try to enforce discipline on her because by the time she arrived she was already a young adult, soon to be nineteen years old. She did not want to obey our rules, and as an act of rebellion, Patricia began discussing our family business with church members and non-Christians. She was uncontrollable.

In Patricia's rebellious state of mind, she left our home for the world. She did not inform us of where she was going and never called to let us know she was all right. There was no communication between us. Although we were sick with worry and were praying constantly for her safety, an opportunity presented itself with my job to further my career, so my wife and I made the decision to purchase a home in Connecticut and move there.

For years we did not hear from Patricia. Then one Saturday morning I received a phone call, and on the other end of the line was a familiar female voice.

"Hi, Dad."

I said, "Is that you, Patricia?"

We talked for a long while. A few weeks later, Patricia came to Connecticut to visit, with her second husband and young son. We knew she was trying to get back to her former position in our lives.

Looking back, I see our lives were full of confusion. At my current place of employment, they were trying to dismiss me from my duties. God is my refuge and strength; a very present help in time of trouble. (See Psalm 46:1.)

Lies and untruths were told about me. The foreman and superintendent stated that I was not capable of carrying out my job. They held a meeting; it included the head of the telephone company, with the foreman and superintendent present. For my support I brought with me a member of the telephone workers' union. They presented their accusations of me being incapable of carrying out the duties of my position, and I was able to disprove their claims and provide supporting evidence to show that I was very capable of carrying out those duties.

John, my foreman, told me a story a month prior that I brought up in the meeting to show that their attempts to fire me were premeditated. John denied having told me this story. The story was of an athletic man who went to Africa and was in the wilderness. A lion began to chase this man, and he ran on the land, but he saw that the lion was catching up on him. He spotted a tree that had a branch, and he jumped up and grabbed onto the branch and was able to escape the lion. John turned to me and said, "Levy, you'd better jump." He wanted me to quit my job to please him.

Nevertheless, the CEO and upper management of the telephone company were able to determine these were lies after going through all of the facts. The Superintendent was relocated to another branch in New Haven, which brought him a great deal of stress. John, the foreman, remained at our office in Stamford. One day John called me into his office, and when I went in, he was talking on the telephone. I overheard John receiving information that they wanted to fire him, but after considering his length of employment they reconsidered. He was so confused after hearing the news that for a brief moment he did not remember he had called me into his office. When he looked up and saw me, he was frightened because he did not realize that I was there and was embarrassed because I had heard the news he had just received. After he caught himself, he said to me, "You may think I had involvement in trying to have you fired, but it's when you are at the bottom of the totem pole you have to listen to those that are on top of the ladder. Those who were above me gave me those orders."

Not long after that, John was transferred from Stamford to New Haven also. I was invited to the farewell party, but I declined the invitation.

During this time I was demoted from my position as a telephone repairman to a painter at the telephone company. One day while I was painting in the hallway,

I was struck with grief. As I looked around in an empty office, I cried out in a loud voice, "I wish I could die!"

A reply came back in a loud voice: "I wish you would!" I was very frightened because I knew I was alone. I looked everywhere—even in the dropped ceiling—because I wanted to know who was listening to me. I realized God had given me the reply. I was struck with fear because I realized that God was listening in on my every word and deed. God hears every word that we say. And indeed, God wants us to die to everything of this world and be alive to Him in the Spirit. Many of our problems in this world as Christians arise because we will not die to this world.

It wasn't long after all of this that they sent down a new manager, superintendent, and foreman to the Stamford branch I was at. I then had a dream concerning a vision that God gave me of the superintended and foreman. I went up a very high staircase and began to chase two pigs. The pigs were so confused that they ran down the stairs, and the bigger pig fell into the bushes and died there. The other pig cried out and went to the bottom of the stairs because I chased him away. You cannot lose with the plan I use! My previous superintendent had suffered a bad epileptic episode and died. John, my previous foreman, was demoted to a position where he was no longer supervising anyone. This was because of his misdeeds while he was in the New Haven office. He was only permitted to go around and check on equipment. When I retired, they forced John to retire too. I found it odd that he was forced into retirement, as I was much older than he was. No weapon formed against me shall prosper. (See Isaiah 54:17.)

CHAPTER 22

AFTER MY RETIREMENT

After I retired from the telephone company, I moved to Georgia with my wife and one of my two sons. Our elder son, John, decided not to move to Georgia with us. He decided to stay in Connecticut, and consequently he was up there when he died. After the funeral, Patricia, who was in attendance, became very belligerent and disrespectful toward my wife regarding the handling of closing out John's official affairs.

Before we headed back to Georgia, Patricia masterminded a treacherous plan to have me leave my wife and son and move to New York with her and her mother. I said, "No way am I going to let my wife and younger son go to Georgia and I stay behind." Patricia came to visit us on several occasions in Georgia. She tried to concoct a plan to get rid of my wife. She did not like my wife, though it was my wife and I who had sponsored her to come to America. She and her mother had been unashamed to beg us to bring her to America and had promised my wife that she would be obedient and respectful, but unfortunately that was not the case when she finally came here, for she turned against my wife.

Patricia began to tell lies about my wife, whom she despised. She took our personal and private conversations to the church. She wrote home and told her mother various stories that were not true. For example, she told her mother that she could not go to bed before four in the morning, because my wife ate so much and she had to tidy the kitchen afterward. Whatever was done in the privacy of our home was made available to Patricia's mother in Jamaica. My aunt was the one who informed us of what Patricia was doing because Patricia's mother gossiped to my aunt. Patricia was shocked to learn that we had been told of her gossiping and spreading of lies. This went on and on for a while.

One morning while Patricia was in Georgia, my wife's nephew called to inform us that he had a vision that someone was going to stab my wife in the back. And I told him that I had the person right in my house. Patricia was in our home, looking for items to use against my wife. She waited at night until we were asleep to creep downstairs and make food while she rummaged through our mail and personal effects. In the mornings we would find a sink full of dishes and an untidy kitchen. Her response would always be that she was only looking for something to eat. During the time while she was downstairs and we were upstairs, she placed red powder under the bases of our lamps in the guest room where she was staying and in the living room.

Before the powder was discovered, Patricia had gone back to her home in New York. A few days after Patricia's visit, my wife was dusting and noticed the powder under a lamp. Because of the amount and color of this substance, it immediately alarmed my wife because we did not know what it was or who had placed it there. We searched the house and found more of this powder throughout our home. Because of the areas of where the powder was placed and the fact that Patricia was the only visitor we had in our home that had the opportunity to do this, all the evidence pointed to her.

We are not certain of what the powder was or why Patricia spread it throughout our home, but we do know it's associated with evil because of her strong dislike for my wife. To this day I am not sure we have swept up all of the powder. Therefore, we must stay in constant prayer. No weapon formed against me shall prosper. (See Isaiah 54:17.)

CHAPTER 23

THE HALF THAT HAS NEVER BEEN TOLD

Patricia sold her house in New York and made a large profit from the sale. She consulted with me to determine whether she should buy a house outright or finance a home in Georgia. I advised Patricia to buy the house outright, and that is what she did. When it came time for her to move down to Georgia, my wife and I did not make our home available to her, owing to our past experience. She phoned my house to set up a time to return a lock and key she had previously borrowed. I informed her that I did not want her to come back to my house because of her behavior toward my wife and son. So she was no longer welcome in our home. She started to curse my wife over the phone. She said all types of disrespectful things about my wife and blamed her for everything.

One day we heard a knock at the door and when we checked it was Patricia. I asked her what happened; she said she just wanted to introduce me to her new husband. Her husband, his brother, and her mother were in her vehicle. Her husband got out of the car to greet me, but when I said hello, there was no response. I extended my hand and repeated myself, but when I still did not hear a reply, I looked into his eyes and was frightened to see they were snakelike, and when I discovered this, he squeezed my hand and let it go; he never spoke a word. I went to speak to the other passengers in the van and heard Patricia's brother-in-law ask her husband, "Did you get him?" and he said, "Yes!" I did not understand at the time what this meant, so I carried on my conversation with Patricia's mother, telling her how much I loved my daughter and that though I did everything possible that I could for her, she just would not behave.

After every sentence, Patricia's brother-in-law would repeat, "Today is the end of it." If I said, "Good," he would say, "Today is the end of it." If I said, "Bad," he would say, "Today is the end of it."

Patricia's mother exclaimed, "I told you, Patricia. You shouldn't do it!"

After everything I said, Patricia called me a liar. I was shocked to see that Patricia would disrespect me in such a way. When I decided to go back in the house, Patricia embraced me, gave me a kiss, and said, "I love you dad," just as Judas did to Jesus after he betrayed him.

After I said good-bye to them, I bent down to pull a weed out of the lawn. Patricia yelled, "No, no, go straight inside!" As I got to the garage, I noticed that my clematis (a flowering plant), which I take pride in, was beginning to grow out of control, so I started to wrap the plant properly. But Patricia yelled again, "No! Go straight inside!"

After I went inside, I was okay until the following day. I was sitting in my dining room at the table and just started to feel sick. I began to fall; luckily my son Phillip was home from work and was able to catch me as I fell. If he hadn't been there, I don't know what would have happened, because I fell unconscious. My wife took my temperature; it was over 102 degrees Fahrenheit. She called for an ambulance, and after the EMTs assessed my condition, they decided to take me to the emergency room. When they were admitting me, the nurse asked me for my name multiple times. I said it was Jesus Christ every time. They looked as if they thought I was crazy.

I remained in the hospital for almost two weeks. Every night that I was in the hospital, I would perspire so much that my bedclothes would have to be changed. The nurses would always ask why was I perspiring so much, but I could not give them an answer, as I did not know why myself, but prayers were being sent up for me. My wife and son were praying fervently for my recovery. My wife asked her local prayer group to pray, and she also reached out to the Trinity Broadcast Network (TBN). Heaven came through, and I began to recover. I am alive! And they that put their trust in the Lord shall be like Mount Zion, which cannot be moved but abides forever. (See Psalm 125:1.) I can testify to the fact that Jesus Christ is Lord. He hears and answers prayers.

After my stay in the hospital, the doctors could not find anything physically wrong with me that would explain the symptoms I had. When I reflect on what could have possibly caused this illness, how could I forget my daughter, who had caused me so much grief—the one in whom I had invested so much energy, time, and effort, and so many resources. When I brought her from Jamaica to America, it was to provide her an opportunity for a better life. She said this was the place she wanted to come to. When I think back on all of the contributions I made in Patricia's adult life, such as procuring a mortgage for her second home, I feel betrayed by her actions. However, when one is lustful and greedy, one will do anything that is despicable or unjust.

Patricia told me that her mother loaned her money that she could not repay and that her sister was being abusive by running after her with knives. Patricia claimed she was just saving her sister's money for her, when it was the truth that Patricia had taken the money and had no intention of paying it back. One can understand why she wanted to kill me because she is lustful after what is not hers. She is like the queen Athaliah of the Scriptures. She killed all the heirs to the throne so she could reign. (See 2 Kings 11, 2 Chronicles 22:10–23:15). Two stories in the Bible come to mind when I think of my daughter's actions: the story of Absalom wanting to kill his father, David, and the story of Abimelech. Abimelech killed sixty-nine of his seventy lawful brothers. Only one of the brothers escaped. (See 2 Samuel 15:1–37). All of them failed in their quests for power. This is what we are seeing in the world today. Someone may think I am harsh in my condemnation of my daughter, but if only that person knew how much I have spent on my daughter or how much I cared for her, he or she would be crying "Shame!" at her wherever she went. That person would say, "Shame on you, Patricia!"

I can only imagine how God felt when Israel turned their backs on Him. When God saw the birth of Israel, the prophet said that no one cared for Israel, and he was cast out in the open field. God then took Israel and cleansed it from his filth. And he became God's child. (See Genesis 35:10.)

When Israel became renowned, Israel discovered other gods, which were not gods at all but the works of man's hand. God was grieved, and God had to send them away into captivity. There they wept when they remembered what they had done.

> By the rivers of Babylon we sat and
>
> wept when we remembered Zion. There
>
> on the poplars we hung our harps for
>
> there our captors asked us for songs, our
>
> tormentors demanded songs of joy; they
>
> said, "Sing us one of the songs of Zion!"

How can we sing the songs of the Lord while in a foreign land? If I forget you, Jerusalem, may my right hand forget its skill. May my tongue cling to the roof of my mouth if I do not consider Jerusalem my highest joy. Remember Lord what the Edomites did on the day Jerusalem fell. "Tear it down," they cried, "tear it down to its foundations!"

> Daughter Babylon, doomed to destruction,
>
> happy is the one who repays you according
>
> to what you have done to us. Happy is
>
> the one who seizes your infants and
>
> dashes them against rocks. (Psalm 137)

All that saw them in Babylon must have been crying, "Shame on you, Zion! How could you have such a mighty God on your side and yet have stooped so low? Shame on you!" I believe that everyone that sees my daughter would say the same. I prayed for my daughter's infirmities because she had a wart on the side of her right .hand. And when I did, she was cured from her infirmities. I even prayed away a pain she was feeling in her side. She told me that her friends said that if they had a father like me who could pray and heal, they would stick close to me. So shame on you, Patricia! It doesn't matter what she does with her hand of inequity; I am on the Lord's side. I am God's handiwork. I am keeping my eyes on the prize in the sky. I know that He cares for me and that He will see me through. It is because of God's grace that I have forgiven Patricia for all that she has done to my family and me.

Looking back at my visit to hell, I mourn for everyone that is heading for such a place. I do not wish for my enemies to experience such desolation. I would advise all of my readers and everyone else to seek the Lord Jesus Christ while there is still time because the end is near.

CHAPTER 24

THE AMAZING CHAPTER

A young man wanted to go to a carpet mill, for he had heard that this carpet maker was the best in town and his work was magnificent. The young man wanted to see the work that everyone was praising and thought so highly of. One day the young man's father decided he was going to purchase carpet from the carpet maker, so it was the young man's opportunity to go see the man's good works.

As they entered the building, the carpet maker heard the voice of the young man. The carpet maker had been told beforehand that that this young man was going to be paying a visit with his father to purchase some carpet. When he arrived at the building, the young man said he didn't think the building was suitable to produce anything beautiful. His condemnation started from outside. When he entered the building, he noticed an overhead rock that was very large in size. The rock served the purpose of allowing the carpet maker to reach carpets that were big in size. The young man could see only the back side of the miller's latest work and thought that his latest creation was far from beautiful. He was beginning to doubt what he had been hearing about how beautiful the carpet maker's works were.

The carpet maker listened to the young man speak negatively about his works of art. He invited the young man to come upstairs to see the front side of the carpet, thinking that might change his opinion.

The young man gingerly went upstairs and waited to see if he would be wowed. He thought to himself, *How can this man be proclaimed as the best carpet maker around?*

The young man's father was waiting downstairs to hear the delight in his son's voice. However, the father heard his son's voice saying in amazement, "Oh my God! Oh my God! I can't believe it." He didn't hear another word, but he heard his son running back downstairs. When his son reached him he said, "Daddy you have to come and see for yourself. This is the half that has never been told. I have seen what you have said and much, much more. The carpets are so beautiful that I don't know who is going to walk on them. And furthermore, you can't buy them, Daddy. They will be too expensive. Isn't it true that the half of the beauty of heaven has never been told to us? To prove it you have to go and look for yourself. One has to have faith in it, and faith for the Maker that is up there.

"Jesus said, 'I am gone to prepare a place for you, and if I go, I will come again and receive you unto Myself, that where I am you might be there also.' To miss heaven is to miss the glory and the beauty of eternal life. We all have an invitation to come up higher, and it's up to us to accept the invitation, that we might be stuck with the beauty of heaven forever; for heaven is a beautiful place, and I am delighted to be a member of heaven, for I am in the family of God. I am going to see that place one of these days in all its beauty and in all its glory. I must see the face of what is on top of this carpet. I've got to be there and will be there when the saints are marching in. Jesus gave me the invitation. I have accepted it gladly."

I would like to say that "God is my refuge and strength, a very present help in times of trouble; therefore I will not fear what man can do unto me". (Psalm 46:1.)

Unto Him that is able to keep us from falling and present faultless before His eternal throne, I raise my hands that everything that I say is true and I am not guilty of any conspiracy. To Him be the glory. Halleluiah! Forever and ever! Amen!

To all of my brothers and sisters in the Lord, Trinity Broadcasting Network (TBN), relatives, friends, my local church, and community, I would like to thank you for your outpouring of love, spiritual support, and prayers throughout the years for my family and me, especially during the period of my illness.

I would like to give thanks and adoration to Sister Evadne Matthews for her kindness during this journey of typing what God gave to me. May God ever bless her and her family.

About the Author

Rev. Levi Russell is a dedicated servant of the Lord wishing to point souls in the right direction for everlasting life beyond this world. He is devoted husband and father who has ministered to many lives.

Printed in the United States
By Bookmasters